Collaborating for
―――――――――
EDITED BY PEGGY HOL......

The Organization Workshop

BARRY OSHRY
AND TOM DEVANE

BERRETT
BK COMMUNICATIONS
KOEHLER

Copyright © 1999 by Barry Oshry and Tom Devane

All rights reserved. No part of this publication may be reproduced, distributed, or transmitted in any form or by any means, including photocopying, recording, or other electronic or mechanical method, without the prior written permission of the publisher, except in the case of brief quotations embodied in critical reviews. For permissions requests, write to the publisher, addressed "Attention: Permissions Coordinator," at the address below:

Berrett-Koehler Communications, Inc.
450 Sansome Street, Suite 1200
San Francisco, CA 94111-3320

ORDERING INFORMATION

Please send orders to Berrett-Koehler Communications, P.O. Box 565, Williston, VT 05495. Or place your order by calling 800-929-2929, faxing 802-864-7626, or visiting www.bkconnection.com.
Special discounts are available on quantity purchases. For details, call 800-929-2929. See the back of this booklet for more information and an order form.

Printed in the United States of America
on acid-free and recycled paper.

CONTENTS

Introduction   1
   Voices That Count: Realizing the Potential of Change
   Peggy Holman and Tom Devane

The Organization Workshop   7
   The Basics   11
   Getting Started   14
   Roles and Responsibilities   16
   Impact on Power and Authority   16
   Conditions for Success   18
   Theoretical Basis   19
   Sustaining the Results   21
   Some Final Comments   21

Notes   24

Resources   25
   Where to Go for More Information

Questions for Thinking Aloud   27

The Authors   30

INTRODUCTION

Voices That Count:
Realizing the Potential of Change

Peggy Holman and Tom Devane

As seen through the lens of history, change is inevitable. Just look at any history book. Everything from fashions to attitudes has changed dramatically through the years. Change reflects underlying shifts in values and expectations of the times. Gutenberg's invention of the movable type printing press in the fifteenth century, for example, bolstered the developing humanism of the Renaissance. The new technology complemented the emerging emphasis on individual expression that brought new developments in music, art, and literature. Economic and political shifts paralleled the changing tastes in the arts, creating a prosperous and innovative age—a stark contrast to the preceding Middle Ages.

On the surface, technology enables greater freedom and prosperity. Yet this century has overwhelmed us with new technologies: automobiles, airplanes, radios, televisions, telephones, computers, the Internet. What distinguishes change today is the turbulence created by the breathtaking pace required to assimilate its effects.

In terms of social change, one trend is clear: People are demanding a greater voice in running their own lives. Demonstrated by the American Revolution and affirmed more recently in the fall of the Berlin Wall, the riots in Tiananmen Square, the social unrest in Indonesia, and the redistribution of power in South Africa, this dramatic shift in values and expectations creates enormous potential for positive change today.

So, why does change have such a bad reputation?

One reason is that change introduces uncertainty. While change holds the possibility of good things happening, 80 percent of us see only its negative aspects.[1] And even when people acknowledge their current situation is far from perfect, given the choice between the devil they know or the devil they don't, most opt for the former. The remedy we are learning is to involve people in creating a picture of a better future. Most of us are drawn toward the excitement and possibility of change and move past our fear of the unknown.

Another reason we are wary of change is that it can create winners and losers. Clearly the British were not happy campers at the end of the American Revolution. In corporations, similar battle lines are often drawn between those with something to lose and those with something to gain. The real challenge is to view the change *systemically* and ask what's best for both parties in the post-change environment.

Finally, many people have real data that change is bad for them. These change survivors know that "flavor of the month" change initiatives generally fall disappointingly short. In our organizations and communities, many people have experienced the results of botched attempts at transformational change. Like the cat that jumps on a hot stove only once, it's simple human nature to avoid situations that cause pain. And let's face it, enough change efforts have failed to create plenty of cynicism over the past ten years. For these people, something had better "smell" completely different if they're going to allow themselves to care.

Ironically, as demands for greater involvement in our organizations increased, leaders of many well-publicized, large-scale change efforts moved the other way and totally ignored people. They chose instead to focus on more visible and seemingly easier-to-manage components such as information technology, strategic architectures, and business processes. Indeed, "Downsize" was a ubiquitous battle cry of the nineties. According to a 1996 *New York Times* poll, "Nearly three-quarters of all households have had a close encounter with layoffs since 1980. In one-third of all households, a family member has lost a job, and nearly 40 percent more know a relative, friend, or neighbor who was laid off."[2] The individual impact has been apparent in the increased stress, longer working hours, and reduced sense of job security chronicled in virtually every recent book and article on change.

To paraphrase Winston Churchill, "Never before in the field of human endeavors was so much screwed up by so few for so many." By ignoring the need to involve people in something that affects them, many of today's popular change methods have left a bad taste in the mouths of "change targets" (as one popular methodology calls those affected) for *any* type of change. They have also often left behind less effective organizations with fewer people and lower morale. Consequently, even well-intentioned, well-designed change efforts have a hard time getting off the ground.

If an organization or community's leaders *do* recognize that emerging values and rapidly shifting environmental demands call for directly engaging people in change, they often face another challenge. When the fear of uncertainty, the potential for winners and losers, and the history of failures define change, how can they systematically involve people and have some confidence that it will work? That is where this booklet comes in.

A Way Through

This booklet offers an approach that works because it acknowledges the prevailing attitudes toward change. It offers a fresh view based on the possibility of a more desirable future, experience with the whole system, and activities that signal "something different is happening this time." That difference systematically taps the potential of human beings to make themselves, their organizations, and their communities more adaptive and more effective. This approach is based on solid, proven principles for unleashing people's creativity, knowledge, and spirit toward a common purpose.

How can this be? It does so by filling two huge voids that most large-scale change efforts miss. The first improvement is *intelligently involving people* in changing their workplaces and communities. We have learned that creating a collective sense of purpose, sharing information traditionally known only to a few, valuing what people have to contribute, and inviting them to participate in meaningful ways positively affects outcomes. In other words, informed, engaged people can produce dramatic results.

The second improvement is a *systemic* approach to change. By asking "Who's affected? Who has a stake in this?" we begin to recognize that no change happens in isolation. Making the interdependencies explicit enables shifts based on a common view of the whole. We can each play our part while understanding our contribution to the system. We begin to understand that in a change effort the "one-party-wins-and-one-party-loses" perception need not necessarily be the case. When viewed from a systemic perspective, the lines between "winners" and "losers" become meaningless as everyone participates in cocreating the future for the betterment of all. The advantages are enormous: coordinated actions and closer relationships lead to simpler, more effective solutions.

The growing numbers of success stories are beginning to attract attention. Hundreds of examples around the world of dramatic and sustained increases in organization and community performance now exist.[3] With such great potential, why isn't everyone operating this way? The catch with high-involvement, systemic change is that more people have their say. Until traditional managers are ready to say yes to that, no matter how stunning the achievements of others, these approaches will remain out of reach for most and a competitive advantage for a few.

Our Purpose

This booklet describes an approach that has helped others achieve dramatic, sustainable results in their organization or communities. Our purpose is to provide basic information that you can use to decide whether this approach is right for you. We give you an overview including an illustrative story, answers to frequently asked questions and tips for getting started. We've also given you discussion questions for "thinking aloud" with others and a variety of references to learn more.

There is ample evidence that when high involvement and a system-wide approach are used, the potential for unimagined results is within reach. As Goethe so eloquently reminds us, "Whatever you can do or dream you can, begin it. Boldness has genius, power, and magic in it."

What are you waiting for?

Customers Customers

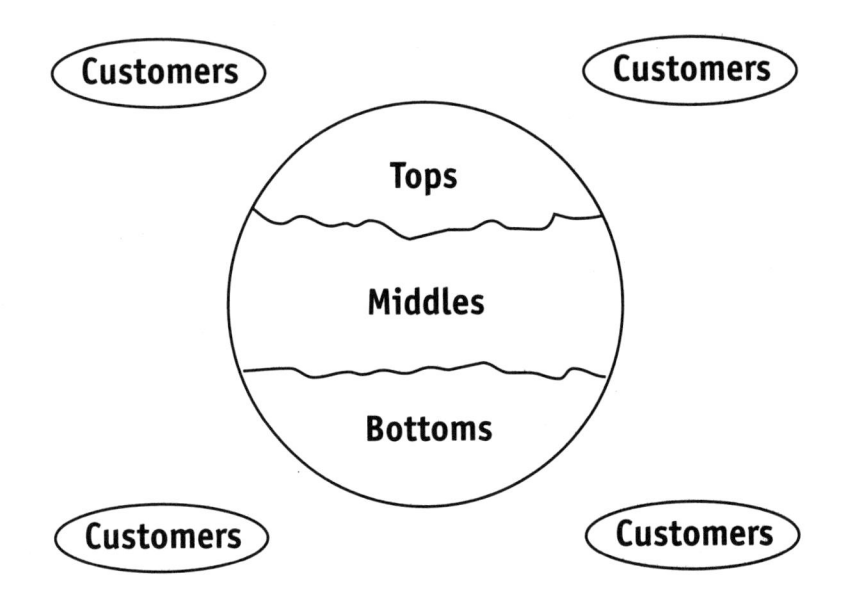

Tops

Middles

Bottoms

Customers Customers

The Organization Workshop

I can see clearly now, the rain is gone,
I can see all obstacles in my way
Gone are the dark clouds that had me blind
It's gonna be a bright, bright sun-shiny day.

—JOHNNY NASH

Between 7:30 and 8:00 A.M., 50 workshop participants arrived at the conference center nestled among pine trees in a rural setting. In the room were some senior executives, middle managers, and frontline workers. There was a high level of anticipation in the room. Though the participants had been briefed before the workshop, there was a lot of animated conversation because the participants didn't quite know what to expect. The California-based H-Tech Company is a 5,000-person high-tech manufacturing organization that was seeking to change its organizational culture. Its target was a culture with more entrepreneurism, less blame, more individual responsibility, and greater partnership across organizational lines.

At 8:00 sharp, the participants were assigned to one of four groups: Tops, Middles, Bottoms, and Customers.

In this exercise, Tops had overall responsibility for the organization, Bottoms were the frontline producers or servicers, Middles each had responsibility for a Bottom group, and Customers and potential Customers had projects for the organization to work on for money. Participants were randomly assigned to positions (except client-organization Tops, who were assigned as Bottoms or Customers).

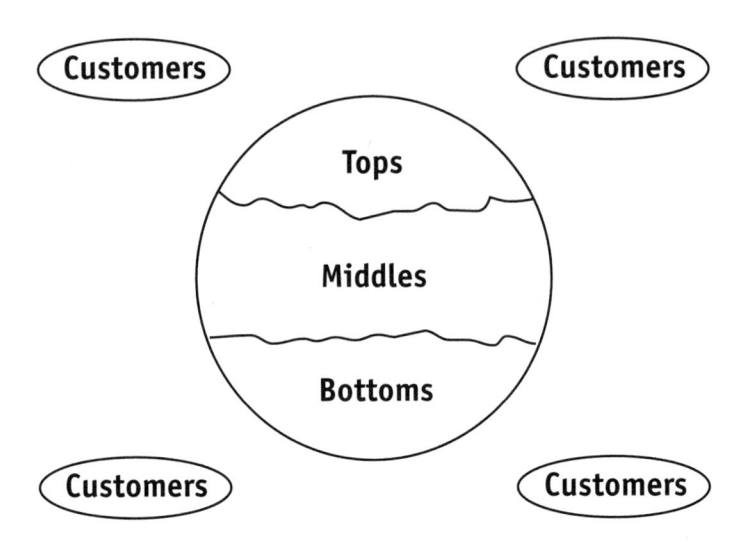

Figure 1. The Four Groups

The first exercise lasted the entire morning. Periodically, action halted and members held a Time Out of Time (TOOT). The TOOT's purpose was for people to talk about life in their positions—what was going on in their world, their issues, their feelings (a mixture of stress, frustration, and anxiety), how they experienced other parts of the system, and what their peer relationships were like. The TOOTs shed light on what was happening in the exercise, but more important, the TOOTs began to illuminate issues that participants were experiencing in their change efforts at their company. For this group, as is almost universal, this was a turning point personally and organizationally. People recognized that this exercise—which was supposed to be very different from their organization—was in fact very much like their organization in the kind of frustration people were experiencing, the misunderstandings that were developing, and the issues people at all levels were facing. From this point, we began to do high-leverage systemic work.

Though the first organizational exercise was completed before lunch, during lunch participants continued to replay the morning's events and their learning. One participant commented on the usefulness of the new framework for highlighting the differing worlds of Tops, Middles, Bottoms, and Customers. She noted how, in her own organization, the conditions of Tops, Middles, Bottoms, and Customers seemed even more aggravated as a result of heightened competition, globalization, increasing workforce diversity, and rapidly changing technology. These conditions led people to make even worse interpersonal choices when trying to partner with others inside and outside the organization.

Table 1 shows what the participants experienced in the exercise that matched what they were experiencing in organizational life.

At 1:00 P.M., everyone was back in the conference room and ready to continue exploring the framework for understanding the worlds of Tops, Middles, Bottoms, and Customers. It was time for a different

Position	Condition	Description
Tops	Overload	Complexity and responsibility; lots of issues, unpredictable issues, issues that aren't dealt with elsewhere; responsibility for the whole system
Middles	Crunch	Feeling of being pulled between differing and often conflicting demands and priorities of Tops and Bottoms; being pulled apart from each other
Bottoms	Disregard	Problems with their condition and with the system; the sense that Tops or Middles ought to fix problems but do not
Customers	Neglect	Products and services not coming fast enough or with acceptable quality or price; inadequate organizational responsiveness

Table 1. Comparison of Participants' Experience with Exercise and with Organizational Life

organizational exercise. In this second exercise all those who were Tops, Middles, and Customers became Bottoms. (The workshop facilitator still kept real-life Tops from being Tops.)

When the participants learned their new positions, we took a few minutes to explore their feelings about them. As usual in the workshops, ex-Tops who were now Bottoms expressed relief; ex-Bottoms who had become Tops were already feeling the stress and tension of responsibility. (It was a moment of humility for some Bottoms who had spent energy in the morning criticizing Tops to find themselves in a Top seat.) Customers reported feeling separateness from the organization. New Middles weren't sure how they felt. Their general sense was that they had no control over what their life would be, that their experience would depend on the actions of Tops, Bottoms, and Customers.

Before proceeding with the second exercise, participants were presented with a strategic framework that helped them see why organizations—despite good intentions and high quality processes—keep falling into the same self-limiting patterns. And they were presented with principles and concrete strategies for creating healthier, more effective systems. Armed with their new "system sight," they began the second exercise, again with a TOOT in the middle to examine the issues. As in many other Organization Workshops, the second exercise was a major leap forward in productivity, creativity, and customer and member satisfaction. Less energy was spent on finger-pointing, blame, withdrawal, and waiting for others to fix things. The group demonstrated more self-responsibility, more understanding and tolerance for others, and more energy focused on the work of the system. Though sometimes the second exercise repeats the difficulties of the first (which itself can be a valuable learning experience), this was not the case for H-Tech, whose employees' performance improved considerably.

In the afternoon exercise, the participants had another organizational-system revelation: *All of us in organizational life—regardless of our level, title, or function—are at times Top/Middle/Bottom/Customer. In some interactions we are Top, in others Bottom, in others Middle, and in others Customer.*

Participants commented on how interesting it was that no matter what their organizational position was (e.g., vice president of manufacturing, sales manager, or junior design engineer), how they experienced problems and crafted responses was more a function of the condition they were in at that moment (Top, Middle, Bottom, or Customer). Just two weeks before the workshop, Mark, a junior design engineer, was the project manager for a small technology project. On this project Mark didn't feel the oppressed, never-listened-to feelings typically associated with being a Bottom. Instead, he felt overwhelmed by complexity, the amount of work, and his responsibility to make sure it got done—the classic feelings of a Top! Why did the junior design engineer have these feelings? Because even though he was low on the organizational ladder, on this project his *condition* was that of a Top.

We call the previous lack of knowledge about organizational processes and interactions *system blindness*. It is our intention in the workshop to convert system blindness to *system sight*.

By the end of the day, participants reported various insights into increasingly successful partnering—both within the organization and with customers—to achieve the organization's overall objectives. At the day's close, participants left emotionally charged, anxious to practice their new learning.

Four months later, the CEO reported that the initial Organization Workshop and follow-up workshops had a dramatic effect on the ways people interacted, positively affecting their performance. Customer satisfaction went way up, and the company significantly decreased new-product development time.

The Basics

The Organization Workshop (OW) is a group learning session in which participants experience universal conditions, traps, and dilemmas of organizational life. By learning firsthand about these traps, along with solid theory on avoiding them, participants emerge with concepts, methods, and a common language to improve their interaction in any organization.

What exactly do we mean by "improving interaction"? We mean that participants learn to form partnerships for higher performance. The partnership-enhancing experiences and learning make it possible for individuals, groups, and entire organizations to operate more effectively and efficiently toward their goals. The workshop focuses on *all* forms of partnerships: higher-level to lower-level partnerships, lateral partnerships spanning organizational units, and supplier-to-customer partnerships.

So how does the Organization Workshop help create conditions for organizations to achieve their goals by improving the way people interact? This is accomplished by helping people open their eyes to organizational processes and interactions about which they were previously unaware. But opening people's eyes is not enough—the Organization Workshop provides people with new choices about how to act with their newfound system sight.

One could say that the purpose of the OW is to demonstrate why—despite our good intentions, well-trained people, and quality processes—our organization initiatives regularly fall short of our expectations. The reason for this depressing phenomenon is that, although we spend much of our lives in organizations and other social systems, we tend not to understand the system processes of which we are a part. The costs of this system blindness are misunderstanding and conflict within and across organizational lines, decreased motivation and initiative, the breakdown of promising partnerships, misplaced energy, poor customer service, and more.

In the Organization Workshop, participants directly experience the costs of system blindness—the costs to them personally and to the organization—and they experience the organizational power as well as the personal liberation, creativity, and empowerment that come from moving from system blindness to system sight.

Rolling out new principles to an entire organization is a challenge with any organizational-transformation effort. If an organization uses OWs as a change platform, the most effective transformations occur when everyone experiences an OW. One strategy has been to develop a cadre of skilled in-house facilitators who can then roll out the workshop through the organization. Another approach is to have a core group—preferably the most influential formal and informal leaders—experience the workshop first. These people can disseminate the principles by conducting discussions with other organization members. Another strategy companies have used is to conduct book discussions on this topic.

Organizations have reported a variety of outcomes, including reduced cycle times, improved quality, lower costs, and higher cus-

System Blindness	System Sight
• We lose focus on the organization's overall objectives and engage in energy-draining peripheral activities that do not directly meet strategic objectives	• We stay focused on activities that directly support the organization's objectives and strategies
	• We have some empathy and understanding for others
• We make up stories about other people's actions (in our stories we are the hero or the victim, never the villain)	• We don't take their actions personally
	• We don't get "hooked" by their actions
• We evaluate others as malicious, insensitive, incompetent	• We stay focused on what it is we are trying to make happen
• We take others' actions personally, as if they are acts against us	• We are strategic
• We react—get mad, get even, withdraw	• We take others' worlds and pressures into account
• That is the end of partnership	• We stay in partnership

Table 2. Comparison of System Blindness and System Sight

tomer service levels. While the Organization Workshop does not specifically address any of these improvement areas, it *creates conditions* for realizing improvements by improving system sight.

The Organization Workshop helps organizations move from weak to powerful organizational systems—ones in which the organizational system gets what it needs, and individuals get what *they* need.

Getting Started

If an organization is considering using the Organization Workshop as a foundation for a change strategy, here are a few things to keep in mind:

- The people who experience the Organization Workshop are the ones who best grasp the concepts and practices for higher performance through partnership. People who hear or read about the concepts are less likely to have the new choices and principles "hardwired" for the split-second decisions required in today's fast-changing world.
- It's critical that senior management attends. Sending others to the workshop to "fix them" doesn't work; senior management is a part of the system that must be addressed to reach higher performance levels.
- Don't try to improve one part of the organization at a time. That is, don't spend six months trying to make frontline workers more effective, then move to middle management, then senior management, and then customer relationships. For the organizational system to work better, all components— Tops, Middles, Bottoms, and Customers—need to exercise system sight choices and improve their performance.

The Organization Workshop has been used in a wide variety of settings for diverse purposes:

THE ORGANIZATION WORKSHOP 15

Use	Some Details
Act as *the* vehicle for a large-scale culture change	A high-tech manufacturing organization of more than 5,000 people began with a cross-level pilot, then introduced a program for the president and his direct reports, and then cascaded the program through the workforce.
Create a values-driven organization	A CEO used the OW to test and embed new organizational values in the face of day-to-day pressures experienced at the top, bottom, and middle of the organization.
Change organizational culture in partnership with other change methods	Aikido and the OW had a powerful combined effect on 700 managers, who brought the principles to their day-to-day efforts. The OW has also been used with Search Conferences and Participative Design Workshops to help organizations reach higher financial performance, operating performance, and intrinsic motivation.
Make new teams as effective as possible, as quickly as possible	One manager uses an OW as a shared experience every time he starts a project, to create mutual understanding and common language and to avoid wasting energy on the usual system blindness.
Help post–Cold War organizations move their new agendas forward	As they shift priorities and directions, these organizations find it useful to understand the traps and opportunities associated with Top, Middle, Bottom, and Customer conditions.
Improve cross-functional team effectiveness	The workshop has been used to smooth relationships and create partnerships within and among cross-functional teams in numerous high-tech and service industries.
Strengthen the role of middle managers in culture-change efforts	In virtually any large-scale change effort—Reengineering, TQM, Self-Managed Work Teams—change is most difficult for the Middle group. Organizations find that the workshop helps middle managers think and behave in ways that support the new direction.
Develop managers into system leaders	In one government agency, the workshop is used to groom middle managers into systemic-thinking senior managers.
Create executive-development programs	Numerous companies use the workshop to create a well-functioning, cohesive, interdependent executive team—not a collection of individuals—that performs at the highest level.

Table 3. Uses of the Organization Workshop

Roles and Responsibilities

The table below describes the key roles and responsibilities before, during, and after the Organization Workshop:

	Pre-Workshop	Workshop	Post-Workshop
Sponsor	Authorize time and budget for the OW	Actively participate	Support and live the language and concepts learned
Designer/ Facilitator	Develop workshop-agenda customizations to fit the organization's needs; conduct a pre-OW briefing session	Conduct the workshop, keep time, provide information on theory and actions facilitate debriefing sessions (TOOTs)	Not always necessary; depends upon the organization's needs
Participants	Attend pre-OW briefing session on workshop purposes and methods	Actively participate	Support and live the language and concepts learned

Table 4. Roles and Responsibilities

Impact on Power and Authority

When viewed from an organizational-chart perspective (the traditional lines-and-boxes relationships), it's possible to say there is no shift in power and authority. The lines and boxes on the organization chart haven't changed. However, when viewed from the perspective of how people choose to interact in an organizational setting, the shift in power and authority can be impressive. Generally, we see the shifts identified in Table 5.

Individuals become aware of, and practice, these new behaviors in the OW. They bring them to their everyday life as conscious choices. While the official organizational structure may not change, the behaviors (and subsequent performance) most often improve dramatically.

Perhaps more dramatic than mere shifts in power and authority are

For...	The general trend is to...	Examples
Tops	create more responsibility throughout the system than before	• Involve others in big decisions such as setting strategic direction and funding large capital projects • Invest in training for people to perform tasks previously done by senior management
Middles	maintain independence of thought and action	• Coach Bottoms seeking to influence Tops • Filter or screen ideas Tops want to implement that affect Bottoms
Bottoms	accept responsibility for their condition and the condition of the entire system	• Propose plans for bettering the entire organization, instead of those that might better their department or career • Constantly think of how consequences of their actions affect the organization's big picture
Customers	get more involved in the delivery of goods and services	• Help design the goods/services delivery process • Enter the process early as a partner, instead of late as a judge

Table 5. Shifts in Power and Authority

the fundamental shifts in the nature of participants' being. It's easy to deal with the concepts and principles glibly: "Oh yes, I see. There's system blindness and there's system sight. I could go this way or that way." Yet it's not as simple as that, which is why we use experiential exercises where we face these choices in action: "In theory, I'm not a Top who loves responsibility, but in the world of action, when a crisis hits—*Whooosh!!*—there I go into blind reflex." "In theory, I'm not one of those whining, complaining Bottoms, and then they (Tops or Middles) do something outrageous and—*Whooosh!!*—there I am, the oppressed Bottom."

We work with people to be clear about the attraction of system blindness: "It's easy; it takes no thought; my friends do it; the causes of my problems always lie outside of myself in other people or circumstance; I'm the hero of all the stories I make up" and so forth. "Why would I want to give all of that up?" We address this fundamental question as our workshop day ends.

What is it that we need to give up, let go of, to consistently use system sight as Tops, Middles, Bottoms, and Customers? This question lies at the core of our change efforts!

We need to scrutinize the control issues that we experience as Tops, the dependency and blame we need to let go of as Bottoms, the overresponsiveness (dancing to every tune that's called, when it's called) that we need to give up to find our independent voices in the Middle, and the distance and feeling of entitlement we need to let go of as Customers. What's the payoff of these behaviors for us, and is it worth it? It can be insightful—and also disconcerting for some—to view the workshop as the end of innocence. Once you've been through it, the option of blindness no longer exists. You are left with awareness and choice.

Conditions for Success

We've talked about when you should use the workshop, but when shouldn't you use it? When

- the Tops aren't present. If the workshop is a systems-change intervention, it makes no sense to do unless the Tops participate. To do otherwise is to reinforce Bottom-ness: "It's just something *they* are doing to us again, as if we're the problem";
- participants have not been adequately informed in advance of the workshop purposes and methods;
- the workshop purposes are not clearly connected to a current system agenda.

Theoretical Basis

Barry Oshry, creator of the OW, describes its theoretical roots:

> In 1960, while at NTL Institute, I discovered the power of *experiential learning:* if you want to learn about groups, create a group and study its processes. Phase I began as I extended this concept to the study of organizations. At Boston University's School of Management, where I was teaching, my graduate assistants and I created organization exercises for 240 undergraduates in a Human Relations and Organizational Behavior course. In parallel, several colleagues and I began experimenting with organization exercises as part of NTL's Management Work Conference.
>
> I entered Phase II as I noticed regularities in the ways Tops, Middles, and Bottoms experienced themselves and one another, even though people were randomly assigned to positions during the exercises. My early writing was descriptive—pictures of the unique stresses and predictable interaction difficulties of Tops, Middles, Bottoms, and Customers. This still left the questions, So what? What are the action implications of this?
>
> Phase III came with the discovery of *mutants,* rare yet highly effective actions taken by Tops, Middles, Bottoms, and Customers. These mutants helped clarify what else is possible.
>
> Evolving over 30 years, these three elements have formed the essence of my work: *experiential designs* that make learning visceral; *descriptive clarity,* an awareness of how organizations usually function; and the *alternative choices* we have for creating more powerful human systems.
>
> The key principles guiding the workshop are as follows:

Principle	Expanded Description
Often what we think is personal really isn't.	When we don't understand other people's "worlds" and the issues they are struggling with, we take their actions personally, as if they are acts against us.
Often what we think is situational really isn't.	Usually when people assert, "It's just the way this organization is," they are playing out their scripts as Tops, Middles, Bottoms, and Customers and becoming uncomfortable because those scripts aren't getting them what they really want or what the organization really needs.
All organizational systems have common characteristics, predictable conditions, predictable traps, and high-leverage opportunities to avoid the traps.	Predictable conditions in each organizational space have associated traps. There are ways out of these traps, and participants practice them in the workshop. These traps may not always be present, but they happen with such regularity that we should not be surprised when we see them, even among friends and colleagues.
For the organizational system to perform better, all the parts must perform better.	For conditions to get better for the whole organization, • Tops must distribute responsibility, *and* • Middles must remain independent in thought and action, *and* • Bottoms must take responsibility for their condition and the condition of the entire system, *and* • Customers must become more actively involved in the delivery process. If only one or two of the above happen, the system's performance will not substantially improve.
Reengineering, TQM, and other popular involvement initiatives will fail unless they look at the processes of systems and the roles people do play and could play in those processes.	During the last 30 years of various improvement programs, common conditions and predictable responses continue to be major improvement barriers. This holds true across all improvement efforts unless system sight is specifically addressed. Successful reengineering and TQM efforts have explicitly or implicitly addressed system sight.
Experience is the best teacher.	That's why teaching occurs through exercises in the workshop.

Table 6. Organization Workshop Principles

Sustaining the Results

A series of Organization Workshops can have a powerful effect on an organization's culture. One definition of culture is the core beliefs and assumptions that people use to guide their choices. By choosing beliefs and assumptions that embrace system sight, individuals make a fundamental shift in the very nature of their being. They *think* differently about organizational interactions and consequently *behave* differently.

An important sustaining aspect of the workshop is the new language it gives people. If we accept the proposition that we use language to create our own reality, it follows that one of the highest-leverage actions available is the act of giving someone a new language. This impacts how people talk to each other and, more important, how they talk to themselves. It's not uncommon for the simple yet powerful workshop language to remain with people for years. Walking down the hall years after a workshop, it's not uncommon to hear "You're being a typical Middle—get out of that situation and let the two parties sort it out" or "You're certainly being a whining Bottom today. Why don't you do something about that problem that makes it better for you and the organization?"

Some Final Comments

How Does This Method Relate to Change?

A notable distinction of the Organization Workshop is that it puts participants into an exercise outside their daily work life. While this method doesn't deal with changing organizational structures, planning processes, or other specific organizational issues, its power lies in another, perhaps more subtle but equally powerful realm. This method changes how people think and interact. This perspective has tremendous potential for significant, sustainable change. After a workshop, managers no longer try to manage people and events; rather, they attempt to manage conditions.

What Are Some Common Misunderstandings About This Method?

One misunderstanding is that the workshop—with its model of Tops, Middles, Bottoms, and Customers—reinforces hierarchy rather than diminishes it. The workshop focuses on relationship patterns that exist in all organizations and are likely to exist in all future organizations, whether flat and participative or hierarchical and bureaucratic. Bureaucratic hierarchy is reinforced when we are blind to these patterns and is diminished when we recognize and manage them.

Another misunderstanding is that the workshop exercises are role-playing sessions in which people are instructed how to act in Top/Middle/Bottom/Customer positions, thus learning how to behave better in their jobs. The exercises are *not* role-play sessions; there are no parts that people are instructed to play. People simply deal with the conditions in which they find themselves. The exercises are constructed so that whoever enters a particular position will experience the conditions of that position *in all organizations:* Tops experience overload, Bottoms experience disregard, Middles crunch, and Customers neglect. Participants don't need to be instructed to behave in a certain way when faced with typical Top, Middle, Bottom, and Customer conditions—they do so by reflex. Instructing people to role-play would be counterproductive to their self-discovery process about what works and what doesn't work.

Another common misunderstanding is that the workshop is a simulation. It's not. We use the word *exercise* to make the point that we are *not* simulating our client's organization, that we use the same exercise with health-care systems, religious institutions, manufacturing and service organizations, government agencies, high-tech firms, schools and colleges. And it's the same exercise we've used (sometimes in translation) in Central America, Australia, Germany, the United Kingdom, South Africa, Hong Kong, Singapore, and other locations around the world. To make the systemic point, it is critical that we do not attempt to tailor the exercise to fit any particular client system. The message is "It's not *your* system; it's *systems*."

Other misunderstandings stem from using the term *Bottoms*. It is often culture-change champions who recoil at the term, who don't want to tag their workers "Bottoms" (they prefer "associates," "partners," "team members"). There are three points:

1. The term is not limited to frontline workers; throughout the program and in the workplace, we use it to refer to the "bottomness" we all experience at various times at all levels and in all positions.
2. In our experience, frontline workers have little trouble with the term *Bottom;* it tends to fit much of their experience.
3. We are not advocating calling frontline people "Bottoms" in the workplace.

One- to three-day workshop variations are offered that can include exercises on system leadership, peer relationships among organizational levels, system sight as it relates to diversity issues, and special topics of interest to the participants and the organization.

Notes

[1] Oakley, Ed, and Doug Krug. *Enlightened Leadership.* Denver, Colo.: Stone Tree Publishing, 1991, p. 38.
[2] The *New York Times, The Downsizing of America.* New York: Times Books, 1996.
[3] Holman, Peggy, and Tom Devane, eds. *The Change Handbook: Group Methods for Shaping the Future.* San Francisco: Berrett-Koehler Publishers, 1999. This book contains over twenty such stories of stellar results from high-involvement, systemic change.

RESOURCES

Where to Go for More Information

Since our focus has been to give you an *introduction* to the Organization Workshop, we want you to know where to go for more information. Here are books, Web sites, and other sources that can help you develop a more in-depth understanding. In addition, we have recommended a work that has influenced us.

Organization

Power & Systems
P.O. Box 990288
Prudential Station
Boston, MA 02199-0288
(617) 437-1640
(617) 437-6713 (fax)
boshry18@aol.com (e-mail)
www.powerandsystems.com (Web site)
- The Organization Workshop: one-, two-, and three-day public and in-house sessions
- The Organization Workshop Train the Trainer Program: A five-day intensive workshop to prepare participants to plan and conduct the Organization Workshop
- The Power & Leadership Conference (Power Lab): The six-day intensive program that has provided much of the systemic theory

- Creating Community in the Face of Difference: A four-day intensive workshop examining issues of dominance as they relate to creating community

The Organization Workshop References

Oshry, Barry. *System Leadership: Lessons from the Power Lab.* San Francisco: Berrett-Koehler, 1999.

———. *Seeing Systems: Unlocking the Mysteries of Organizational Life.* San Francisco: Berrett-Koehler, 1995.

———. *In the Middle.* Boston: Power & Systems, 1994.

———. *Space Work.* Boston: Power & Systems, 1992.

———. *The Possibilities of Organization.* Boston: Power & Systems 1986.

Influential Source

Laszlo, Ervin. *The System View of the World: A Holistic Vision for Our Time.* New York: George Braziller, 1972.

Jen please input these questions

Systems Awareness Questions adapted from the authors.

Questions for Thinking Aloud

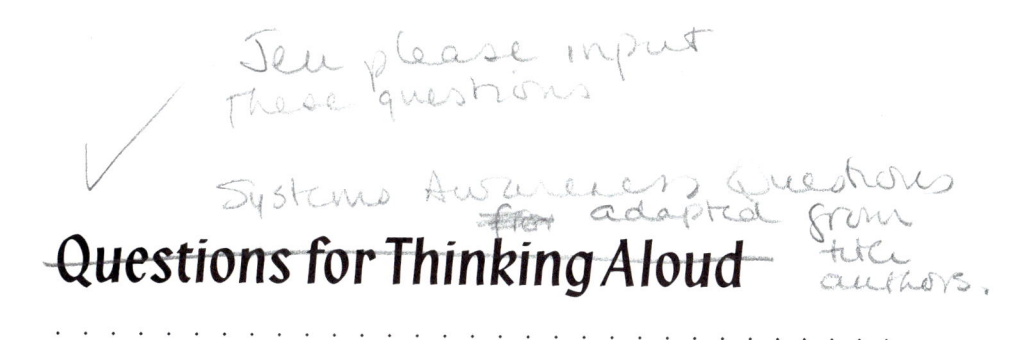

doc/CCMD Phase 2 2002 and 2008/09 file → DORIS debrief questions

To gain additional value from this booklet, consider discussing it with others. Here are some questions you might find useful as you explore the Organization Workshop and its application to your situation.

1. Think of your personal experiences in organizations (a community, corporation, church group, trade association, or any group of people with a formal set of structured relationships). When you've been a Top, Middle, Bottom, or Customer, have you felt the strong gravitational pull of the conditions associated with those positions? (See Table 1 for a list.) Give some examples of your experiences. Have you ever found yourself doing the commonly encountered, counterproductive reflex actions associated with those conditions? Tell some stories about this.

2. It's been said that many of the Organization Workshop principles are just an "advanced form of common sense" and "a blinding flash of the obvious." Why does applying them seem so rare?

3. What do you see as the advantages to addressing organizational problems from the perspective of an individual's position in the system—that is, Top, Middle, Bottom, or Customer—rather than as flaws of an individual's personality?

4. System Blindness (Table 2) is a naturally occurring condition in most organizations. What do you think are the costs of System Blindness to your organization in terms of

- Organizational productivity?
- Personal relationships?
- Your ability to influence others in the organization when you really need to?
- Personal health?
- Effective partnerships within the organization and outside the organization?

5. In the Organization Workshop participants learn to form partnerships for higher performance, replacing the more common dominator-dominated approach. What do you see as the benefits of a partnership approach? Discuss ways that a partnership approach may—or may not—help an organization achieve its goals.

6. The Organization Workshop gives people new language to discuss situations, problems, and solutions. When seeking organizational improvement, why is this such a high-leverage action? That is, why will a little effort make a big difference?

7. In any major transformation[1] middle managers are often cited as either the key blockers to change (in the worst-case scenario) or the key enablers of change (when they're on board and genuinely support the change). Based on what you now know about the natural conditions and reflex actions of Middles, why do you suppose this is so? What impact would Middles who do possess Systems Sight have on a large-scale change effort?

8. Research has shown that the principles of system awareness can improve the working relations of any organization—be it a bureaucratic hierarchy or an empowered organization of self-managing teams. Why do you suppose these principles seem to have such a broad applicability across such a wide range of leadership styles and organizational structures? How might they specifically help your

organization with its given leadership style and organizational structure?

9. How might the Organization Workshop principles be used to help redistribute decision-making authority within an organization? As a reminder, the key principles are
   - Often what we think is personal really isn't.
   - Often what we think is situational really isn't.
   - All organizational systems have common characteristics, predictable conditions, predictable traps, and high-leverage opportunities to avoid the traps.
   - For the organizational system to perform better, all the parts must perform better.
   - Reengineering, TQM, and other popular improvement initiatives will fail unless they look at the processes of systems, and the roles people do play and could play in those processes.
   - Experience is the best teacher.

10. If you determine that an Organization Workshop is appropriate for your organizational objectives and organizational culture, what might be the next steps for you to take to make it happen?

Note

[1] For example, reengineering, organizational restructuring, the implementation of an Enterprise Resource Planning system (such as SAP, Oracle, PeopleSoft), or a Total Quality initiative.

The Authors

Barry Oshry, Ph.D., attended NTL Institute's (then called the National Training Laboratories) first Applied Behavioral Science Intern program in 1960. This began his use of experiential learning to study organizations. While teaching at Boston University's School of Management (then called the College of Business Administration), his continued experimentation led to his book *Power and Position,* a descriptive account of what he was learning. His current practice is based in part on theories about power and his insight into possible alternatives gained through years of conducting workshops. His current books include *The Possibilities of Organization, Space Work, In the Middle, Seeing Systems,* and *Leading Systems: Lessons from the Power Lab.*

Tom Devane helps organizations reach higher levels of financial and human performance. Tom's professional journey has included a number of stops along the way to his current specialty areas of organization and community transformation. Each stop provided an additional piece of the transformation jigsaw puzzle. His key stops—corporate finance, information technology, Total Quality, strategic planning, Reengineering, Organization Development, and leadership effectiveness—combined to create a systemic approach to change that is multifaceted and sustainable. Tom holds bachelor's and master's degrees in finance from the University of Illinois. Prior to founding Premier Integration in 1987, Tom was the practice leader for an international Big Six consulting firm. Before that, he was a regional manager at a Fortune 100 firm. Representative clients include Microsoft, Hewlett-Packard, AT&T, Johnson & Johnson, Lucent Technologies, StorageTek, Weyerhaeuser Company, U S WEST, the state of Colorado, the U.S. Forest Service, and the Republic of South Africa.

Series Editors

Peggy Holman is a writer and consultant who helps organizations achieve cultural transformation. High involvement and a whole-systems perspective characterize her work. Her clients include AT&T Wireless Services, Weyerhaeuser Company, St. Joseph's Medical Center, and the U.S. Department of Labor. Peggy can be reached at (425) 746-6274 or pholman@msn.com.

Tom Devane is an internationally known consultant and speaker specializing in transformation. He helps companies plan and implement transformations that utilize highly participative methods to achieve sustainable change. His clients include Microsoft, Hewlett-Packard, AT&T, Johnson & Johnson, and the Republic of South Africa. Tom can be reached at (303) 898-6172 or tdevane@iex.net.

Collaborating for Change
Peggy Holman and Tom Devane, Editors

The Collaborating for Change booklet series offers concise, comprehensive overviews of 14 leading change strategies in a convenient, inexpensive format. Adapted from chapters in *The Change Handbook*, each booklet is written by the originator of the change strategy or an expert practitioner, and includes

- An example of the strategy in action
- Tips for getting started
- An outline of roles, responsibilities, and relationships
- Conditions for success
- Keys to sustaining results
- Thought-provoking questions for discussion

If you're deciding on a change strategy for your organization and you need a short, focused treatment of several alternatives to distribute to your colleagues, or you've decided on a change strategy and want to disseminate information about it to get everyone on board, the Collaborating for Change booklets are the ideal choice.

◆ SEARCH CONFERENCE
Merrelyn Emery and Tom Devane
Uses open systems principles in strategic planning, thereby creating a well-articulated, achievable future with identifiable goals, a timetable, and action plans for realizing that future.

◆ FUTURE SEARCH
Marvin R. Weisbord and Sandra Janoff
Helps members of an organization or community discover common ground and create self-managed plans to move toward their desired future.

◆ THE CONFERENCE MODEL
Emily M. Axelrod and Richard H. Axelrod
Engages the critical mass needed for success in redesigning organizations and processes, co-creating a vision of the future, improving customer and supplier relationships, or achieving strategic alignment.

◆ THE WHOLE SYSTEMS APPROACH
Cindy Adams and W. A. (Bill) Adams
Creates a world of work where people and organizations thrive and produce outrageous individual and organizational results.

◆ PREFERRED FUTURING
Lawrence L. Lippitt
Mobilizes everyone involved in a human system to envision the future they want and then develop strategies to get there.

- **THE STRATEGIC FORUM**
Chris Soderquist
Answers "Can our strategy achieve our objectives?" by building shared understanding (a mental map) of how the organization or community really works.

- **PARTICIPATIVE DESIGN WORKSHOP**
Merrelyn Emery and Tom Devane
Enables an organization to function in an interrelated structure of self-managing work groups.

- **GEMBA KAIZEN**
Masaaki Imai and Brian Heymans
Builds a culture able to initiate and sustain change by providing skills to improve process, enabling employees to make daily improvements, installing JIT systems and lean process methods in administrative systems, and improving equipment reliability and product quality.

- **THE ORGANIZATION WORKSHOP**
Barry Oshry and Tom Devane
Develops the knowledge and skills of "system sight" that enable us to create partnerships up, down, and across organizational lines.

- **WHOLE-SCALE CHANGE**
Kathleen D. Dannemiller, Sylvia L. James, and Paul D. Tolchinsky
Helps organizations remain successful through fast, deep, and sustainable total system change by bringing members together as one-brain (all seeing the same things) and one-heart (all committed to achieving the same preferred future).

- **OPEN SPACE TECHNOLOGY**
Harrison Owen (with Anne Stadler)
Enables high levels of group interaction and productivity to provide a basis for enhanced organizational function over time.

- **APPRECIATIVE INQUIRY**
David L. Cooperrider and Diana Whitney
Supports full-voiced appreciative participation in order to tap an organization's positive change core and inspire collaborative action that serves the whole system.

- **THINK LIKE A GENIUS PROCESS**
Todd Siler
Helps individuals and organizations go beyond narrow, compartmentalized thinking; improve communication, teamwork, and collaboration; and achieve breakthrough thinking.

- **REAL TIME STRATEGIC CHANGE**
Robert W. Jacobs and Frank McKeown
Uses large, interactive group meetings to rapidly create an organization's preferred future and then sustain it over time.

The Change Handbook
Group Methods for Shaping the Future

Edited by Peggy Holman and Tom Devane

The Change Handbook presents eighteen proven, highly successful change methods that enable organizations and communities of all shapes and sizes to engage and focus the energy and commitment of all their members These diverse participative change approaches, described in detail by their creators and expert practitioners, illustrate how organizations and communities today can achieve and sustain extraordinary results and foster a capacity to handle the inevitable turbulence along the way. By first systematically involving all organizational stakeholders in the change process, and then planning and implementing change simultaneously—in real time—these methods uniquely enable all members to become change agents, active participants in determining their organization's direction and future.

Marvin Weisbord, Merrelyn Emery, Masaaki Imai, Kathie Dannemiller, Harrison Owen, and many other leading thinkers and practitioners of organizational change show how to harness the vision, energy, and enthusiasm of the entire organization—from employees at all levels to key stakeholders to entire communities. In *The Change Handbook* they provide practical answers to frequently asked questions to that you can choose the methods that will work best in your participative change efforts.

> *"In a world where change is the norm, where the effectiveness of organizations is a competitive advantage, and where we have more change methodologies available than most people could absorb in a lifetime, this book has identified how to match the best approach to the situation. While providing structured guidelines for organizational improvement, the authors acknowledge and celebrate the power of creativity and engaged people to provide the energy needed for successful change."*
>
> —S<small>USAN</small> M<small>ERSEREAU</small>, *Vice President,*
> *Organizational Effectiveness, Weyerhaeuser Company*

Paperback original, approx. 450 pages, ISBN 1-57675-058-2
Item no. 50582-605   U.S. $49.95
To order call 800-929-2929 or visit www.bkconnection.com

Collaborating for Change Order Form
Each booklet comes shrinkwrapped in packets of 6

Order in Quantity and Save!
1–4 packets: $45 per packet • 5–9 packets: $40.50 per packet
10–49 packets: $38.25 per packet • 50–99 packets: $36 per packet

# of Packets		Item #	Price
_____	Search Conference	6058X-605	_____
_____	Future Search	60598-605	_____
_____	The Strategic Forum	60601-605	_____
_____	Participative Design Workshop	6061X-605	_____
_____	Gemba Kaizen	60628-605	_____
_____	The Whole Systems Approach	60636-605	_____
_____	Preferred Futuring	60644-605	_____
_____	The Organization Workshop	60652-605	_____
_____	Whole-Scale Change	60660-605	_____
_____	Open Space Technology	60679-605	_____
_____	Appreciative Inquiry	60687-605	_____
_____	The Conference Model	60695-605	_____
_____	Think Like a Genius Process	60709-605	_____
_____	Real Time Strategic Change	60717-605	_____

Shipping and Handling _____
($4.50 for the first packet; $1.50 for each additional packet.)

TOTAL (CA residents add sales tax) $_____

Method of Payment
Orders payable in U.S. dollars. Orders outside U.S. and Canada must be prepaid.

❏ Payment enclosed ❏ Visa ❏ MasterCard ❏ American Express

Card no. _____ Expiration date _____

Signature _____

Name _____ Title _____

Organization _____

Address _____

City/State/Zip _____

Phone (in case we have questions about your order) _____

May we notify you about new Berrett-Koehler products and special offers via e-mail?

E-mail _____

Send Orders to Berrett-Koehler Communications, Inc., P.O. Box 565, Williston, VT 05495 • **Fax** (802) 864-7626 • **Phone** (800) 929-2929 • **Web** www.bkconnection.com